THE SEARCH FOR TRUTH

Prophet Muhammad for Little Hearts

by

SANIYASNAIN KHAN

Goodwordkidz

Helping you build a family of faith

At the age of 25 years, the Prophet Muhammad ﷺ was married to a widow, whose name was Khadijah. She came from the family of merchants. The marriage gave him every opportunity to lead a comfortable life as a wealthy and respected noble man of Makkah.

4

And, indeed, for a few years the Prophet Muhammad ﷺ did lead a calm and quiet life as a merchant.

But he soon gave up all worldly activity
and set himself to searching for the truth.

Instead of meeting people all the time in their homes and at gatherings, and trying to gain for himself a position among the nobility of Makkah, the Prophet Muhammad ﷺ would wander into the barren hills of the desert.

9

He would sit for hours and ponder
over the mysteries of creation.

The vast silence of the desert, with endless sand and sky and, at night, equally endless darkness, alive only with the twinkling of millions and millions of tiny stars, seemed to bring one very close to the Creator.

13

14

Often the Prophet Muhammad ﷺ would stay alone for days in the Cave of Hira, which was on the top of Jabal al-Nur, or the Mountain of Light. It was situated three miles from Makkah.

He would return home only for more supplies of food and water, and then go back to the solitude of nature to pray and meditate.

He would sit there for hours and hours asking the Maker of the heavens and the earth for answers to the questions that surged in his mind.

19

What is man's true role in life? What does the Lord require of us, as His servants? From where does man come, and where will he go after death?

On the twelfth of February, 610 A.D., the Prophet Muhammad ﷺ, now forty years of age, went to the Cave of Hira to spend Ramadan, the traditional month of retreat.

He was sitting all alone in this cave, when he had an extraordinary experience. An angel came to him in human form in the cave and taught him the first few verses of the Quran. Thus Allah appointed him as the final prophet to humanity.